# Special Desserts

❧❧❧❧❧❧❧

# Special Desserts

*Ann Amernick*

ILLUSTRATIONS BY
MELANIE MARDER PARKS

*Clarkson Potter/Publishers*
*New York*

Published by Clarkson Potter/Publishers, 201 East 50th Street,
New York, New York 10022. Member of the Crown Publishing Group.

CLARKSON N. POTTER, POTTER and colophon are trademarks
of Clarkson N. Potter, Inc.

Manufactured in Japan

Design by Jane Treuhaft

LIBRARY OF CONGRESS CATALOGING IN PUBLICATION DATA
Amernick, Ann.
[Special desserts]
Ann Amernick's special desserts / by Ann Amernick.
p.  cm.
Includes index.
1. Desserts.    I. Title.   II. Title: Special desserts.
TX773.A422    1992
641.8′6 — dc20                                      91-32740
                                                          CIP

ISBN: 0-517-57672-4
10  9  8  7  6  5  4  3  2  1
First Edition

For Jay and Dan Amernick,
and Lincoln Mudd,
*with love*

# Contents

## Cakes and Tortes

## Pies and Tarts

# Cookies and Candies
*35*

# Cold Desserts
*51*

# Master Recipes
*67*

# Acknowledgments

&#x265e;&#x265e;&#x265e;&#x265e;&#x265e;&#x265e;&#x265e;

A lthough this is a small book, I have some large thank-yous. My gratitude goes to many people who, over the years, have helped me realize my goals. Perhaps some of these people were just there when I needed help and may not have realized how much their presence and support motivated me in my work.

My thanks to Shirley Wohl, my editor, whose work and direction have kept me from sinking and whose advice has been essential; to her assistant, Bill Nave, for helping with details with such good cheer; to Linda Greider, food writer extraordinaire, who will never know how much her enormous help on *Soufflés* enabled me to write this new book; to George Lang, chef, author, and restaurateur par excellence, who created the path to Clarkson Potter; to Margaret Doubleday, caterer and dedicated cook, who worked with me through the all-nighters without asking for anything, even a thank-you; to Judy Lewis Lustine and Geri Elias, who both provided the much needed shoulder to lean on; to Patrick Musel and Roland Mesnier, two of the three finest and most dedicated pastry chefs I have ever worked with, and whose teachings and guidance were tantamount to leading me into the professional pastry world; to Richard Chirol, the third of those exceptional pastry chefs, without whose inspiration for *Soufflés* I would never have had the opportunity to write *Special Desserts;* to Jean-Louis Pallidan, world-class chef and sharing friend, for the opportunity to work in a true French kitchen and authenticate myself; to Catherine Grove, cook and assistant to Chef Jean-Louis Pallidan, whose recipe testing and writing expertise were indispensable; to the late Anne Crutcher, whose style and class helped raise the level of food appreciation in Washington, D.C.; Patricia Altobello, Deirdre Pierce, Carol Mason, Joan Nathan, Phyllis

Richman, and Lisa Yockelson, the crème de la crème of women in the food world today, for their enthusiasm, encouragement, and appreciation of my work; to my parents, Morris and Helen Silverberg, my aunt, Bee Goldberg, my brothers, David and Alan Silverberg, and my sister and brother-in-law, Abby and Steve Lazinsky, who, during the most difficult times in my life, were there before I even asked; to my two sons, Jay and Dan Amernick, who couldn't be thanked enough in ten books for their patience, their humor, and their warm understanding; and to Lincoln Mudd, whose kindness, generosity, and stalwart presence have enriched every day, and who has taught me the value of valuing.

# Special Desserts

# Introduction

∾∾∾∾∾∾∾

I n 1970, when I was already the mother of two young sons, I went to Europe for the first time. And Paris changed my life. Pastries and desserts had fascinated me ever since I was very young, so to me the beautifully composed pastries that I sampled in Paris were the edible jewels of my childhood dreams. I knew then that creating desserts would be my profession.

When I returned home from that trip, my dessert odyssey began. I experimented with ingredients, I played with oven temperatures. And the cookbooks! From Julia Child to the Time-Life Cooking Series to Paula Peck—just to look at the pictures and imagine making the recipes was inspiring. A few years later, when I began working in such Washington, D.C., restaurants as The Big Cheese, Le Pavillon, Maison Blanche, and Jean-Louis at the Watergate—and even as assistant pastry chef in the White House kitchen during the Carter administration—I found the experience to be unbelievably exciting and rewarding, despite the long hours and sometimes difficult working conditions. Now, after almost twenty years of creating desserts both for restaurants and my own private clientele, I still find it as rewarding as ever.

Over the years, many people have asked for a number of my recipes. For this reason, I have decided to share the most popular by writing this book. The recipes that I have compiled and adapted for the home cook range from the down-home and simple—such as Sour Cream Blueberry Pie and Baked Apple Cake—and the elegant and sophisticated—such as Lime Bavarian and Gâteaux Bretonnes—to desserts that have been longtime favorites of chocolate lovers, including Chocolate Fudge Cake and Viennese Chocolate Fantasy.

These desserts require ingredients of the highest quality and are for those occasions when you're ready to splurge on the real thing. I have made some of the desserts lighter by using less sugar than called for in the original recipes, but without sacrificing any of the taste. Few of the recipes are low in calories, but I feel that a small taste of something delectable is preferable to a large portion of a dessert containing low-fat, ersatz ingredients that render it mediocre, or second-rate at best. Some of the desserts should be cut in thinner slices that will serve a larger number of people and, of course, bring down the calorie count for each. The recipes generally are not difficult; some are more involved than others, but I have tried to make each one easy to follow.

Some of the master recipes make a bit more than is called for in the individual dessert, which I prefer, especially with the toppings and fillings. You'll find that you will work faster when you don't have to stop in the middle of finishing a cake because you didn't make enough frosting, cream, or custard filling beforehand. Most extras can be frozen, to be used at another time. These extras also are handy for last-minute desserts when unexpected company arrives. To be able to whip up a lemon buttercream torte or a chocolate bombe with little advance notice is a breeze when your freezer holds the answers.

## UTENSILS

**Mixer.** An electric mixer is the mainstay of most bakers' kitchens, whether it be a simple hand-held portable or a heavy-duty mixer with various chopping and grinding attachments. The latter type of mixer allows you to mix and whip ingredients or knead doughs, without using as much elbow grease as you would doing these tasks by hand.

**Wire Whisk.** A wire whisk has always been one of the handiest general pieces of equipment in any kitchen. It is excellent for whipping egg whites or heavy cream.

**Bowls.** I recommend using stainless-steel bowls. They conduct both heat and cold, which helps when melting or cooling ingredients in a hot *bain-*

*marie* or in an ice bath — for example, melting chocolate or keeping heavy cream chilled for whipping.

**Bain-Marie.** A *bain-marie* is a water bath for heating or chilling ingredients by using hot or cold water instead of direct heat or refrigeration. It is, in effect, a double boiler that you can create with a large pot and a mixing bowl. I use this method instead of a double boiler because it provides the means for preparing larger volumes. To create a *bain-marie*, fill a pot two-thirds full with hot or ice water, depending upon your needs, and immerse the bowl in the pot. The size of the pot and bowl will depend on the quantity of ingredients. I find that for melting chocolate, stove-top heat isn't necessary. Hot tap water is usually enough to gently melt the chocolate. When a cold bath is needed, for best results, the pot should contain enough ice water to come about one-third of the way up the sides of the bowl. A *bain-marie* is also wonderful for bringing either hot or cold ingredients or mixtures to room temperature.

**Spatulas.** A flexible rubber spatula or scraper is invaluable for folding together ingredients by hand, especially during the final stages of preparing cookie dough. Thin-bladed metal spatulas are excellent for icing cakes. I particularly like a 10-inch offset spatula, which has a bend in the metal like a painter's trowel, making it ideal for leveling off the top of a cake. An 8-inch regular spatula works well for covering the sides. These various spatulas are available at most stores that carry baking supplies.

**Baking Pans.** My recipes call for 8-inch and 10-inch round cake pans as well as various sizes of square or rectangular pans. You'll also need an 8-inch and a 10-inch springform, which is a pan with a mechanism used to release the sides so a cake does not have to be inverted. Springforms are especially handy for mousses and bavarians. For several other recipes you will need an 8-, 9-, or 10-inch false-bottomed fluted tart pan (the bottom detaches and can be removed) as well as 9- and 10-inch pie pans.

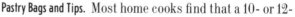

**Pastry Bags and Tips.** Most home cooks find that a 10- or 12-inch bag is the most useful size and easy to handle. In those recipes requiring a pastry bag, I recommend either a ½-inch fluted or star tip and a ½-inch plain tip, except for the ¾-inch plain tip suggested for the Palets aux Raisins. This larger tip prevents the currants from clogging when you're piping out the dough.

**Baking Sheets and Parchment Paper.** Baking sheets can be either flat cookie sheets or sheets with very low sides. You will find, however, that a thicker, higher-quality baking sheet or tray will distribute heat more evenly and allow for more uniform baking. Parchment paper is sometimes used on baking sheets and in cake pans to prevent baked goods from sticking. It is available in rolls in kitchenware shops and department stores. If you use nonstick bakeware, you won't need to use parchment paper.

**Cake Racks.** These metal racks are available in any kitchenware store and are invaluable for cooling cake pans or pie pans after removing them from the oven.

**Citrus Zester or Fine Grater.** Several of the recipes depend on the intense fruity flavor of citrus zest—the colored part of the rind that adds flavor without the bitterness of the white pith. A citrus zester, available at kitchenware shops, is a little implement that peels off small strips of the zest. For tiny morsels of zest, chop the strips with a sharp knife. Zest can also be obtained with a fine grater.

**Pastry Brush.** These come in handy when washing down the sugar crystals that form on the sides of a pot of sugar syrup before it comes to a boil. This is a very important step. Washing down the sides of the pot rinses away any undissolved sugar crystals that might begin a chain reaction, causing an entire batch of candy to crystalize.

**Candy Thermometer.** This is a thermometer specifically designed to be used in candy making and useful for several of the recipes in this book. It can be purchased in kitchenware shops and department stores.

**Rolling Pin.** The larger and heavier the better! I prefer a wooden rolling pin with ball bearings.

**Kitchen Scale.** I recommend a small scale for weighing certain ingredients such as chocolate. Weighing chocolate is more accurate than chopping a cupful, since the chopped chocolate can vary in size and therefore volume.

## TIPS AND TECHNIQUES

Always read a recipe thoroughly before beginning to familiarize yourself with the ingredients and procedure. This will save time later on.

All recipes use large eggs, and all ingredients should be at room temperature unless otherwise stated.

I always recommend beating cookie dough either on the lowest speed of the electric mixer with a paddle attachment or by hand. I also suggest that you finish mixing all doughs by hand. This way, less air is beaten in, resulting in a more tender cookie or pastry. I learned this technique when I was assistant to Roland Mesnier, the acclaimed White House pastry chef.

I have found that rotating cookie sheets in the oven—turning front to back and changing levels—helps distribute the heat evenly. Ideally, baking one sheet at a time keeps them from competing with one another for the oven heat. I follow this advice from Lisa Yockelson, an expert baker and cookbook author.

When making candy, most people feel more comfortable using a candy thermometer to determine the proper temperature of the sugar syrup. Sometimes, however, I find that simply dropping a spoonful of the hot syrup into a glass of ice water and then gathering the syrup between my thumb and forefinger to form a ball is a more reliable method. You can actually feel the firmness of the sugar, be it a soft, firm, or hard ball. Use whatever way suits you best.

# Cakes
## *and*
# Tortes

*Chocolate Fancy Cake*

*Chocolate Fudge Cake*

*"Birdseed" Cake*

*Baked Apple Cake*

*Viennese Chocolate Fantasy*

*Chocolate Raspberry Torte*

*Lemon Buttercream Torte*

*Amaretti Meringue Torte*

*Caramel Nut Torte*

# Chocolate Fancy Cake

*This is a dense, chocolatey cake with a*
*veneer of cocoa powder.*

**[Serves 8 to 10]**

10 ounces bittersweet chocolate
½ cup (1 stick) unsalted butter
½ cup sugar
5 large eggs, separated
2 tablespoons dark rum
⅓ cup ground almonds
Crème Ganache (page 75)
½ cup cocoa

Preheat the oven to 300° F. Butter well an 8-inch cake pan and line the bottom with parchment paper.

Place the chocolate in a double boiler over hot, not boiling, water. When the chocolate is melted, turn off the heat and leave the chocolate over the hot water.

Meanwhile, in a mixing bowl, beat the butter with ¼ cup of the sugar until light and fluffy. Add the egg yolks and beat for 1 minute. Add the rum and the almonds and beat for 2 minutes. In a separate bowl, beat the egg whites until light and foamy while gradually adding the remaining sugar. Continue beating until the whites are stiff and shiny.

Add the melted chocolate to the butter mixture and mix with a rubber spatula until well combined. Fold one-quarter of the chocolate mixture into the egg whites, then fold the egg whites into the chocolate mixture. Fold gently so as not to deflate the meringue.

Pour the mixture into the cake pan and bake about 25 minutes or until a cake tester inserted in the center has some crumbs clinging to it. Cool the cake in the pan for 10 minutes, then carefully turn the cake out onto a plate. Chill while you prepare the topping.

Whip 1½ cups of *ganache* until light and fluffy. Smooth it over the top and sides of the cake. Chill the cake for 1 hour, then sift a thin, even coat of cocoa over the top. With the tip of a sharp knife, score the top of the cake in a diamond pattern. Serve at room temperature. This cake is very rich and a little goes a long way. I have served as many as 12 to 14 very thin slices.

# Chocolate Fudge Cake

*A rich, brownielike cake, this is a favorite*
*for children's birthday parties. The trick is keeping it*
*away from the adults!*

[Serves 15 or more]

10 ounces unsweetened
chocolate

2 cups (4 sticks) unsalted
butter

8 large eggs

3¼ cups sugar

2 teaspoons vanilla extract

2 cups all-purpose flour, sifted

Chocolate Fudge Frosting
(recipe follows)

Preheat the oven to 350° F. Butter an 18 × 11-inch rectangular baking pan. Cut a piece of cardboard into a 19 × 12-inch rectangle (use a box or carton). Cover the rectangle with aluminum foil. Set aside.

Melt the chocolate and butter together in a large metal bowl set on top of a pot of simmering water. When the mixture has melted and is well combined, remove from the heat. Meanwhile, beat the eggs with the sugar until thick and pale yellow (don't worry if the sugar does not seem completely dissolved). Add the chocolate mixture to the egg mixture and stir to combine completely. Add the vanilla. Add the flour one-quarter at a time, mixing well after each addition.

Pour the batter into the prepared pan and bake about 30 to 35 minutes, until a cake tester comes out with a few crumbs clinging to it. Cool the cake in the pan for 10 minutes. Invert it onto the foil-covered cardboard. Frost with Chocolate Fudge Frosting when completely cool. To serve, cut into 2-inch squares.

**Note:** If you prefer, you can frost the cake with 2 cups of heavy cream, whipped and flavored with 1 teaspoon of vanilla extract and 2 tablespoons of confectioners' sugar.

ఈఈఈఈఈఈ

# Chocolate Fudge Frosting

¾ cup sugar
1 cup heavy cream
5 ounces unsweetened chocolate
½ cup (1 stick) unsalted butter
2 teaspoons vanilla extract

Mix the sugar and cream in a 2-quart sauce-pan and bring to a boil. Lower the heat and simmer for 6 minutes. Add the chocolate, butter, and vanilla. Stir until the chocolate and butter have melted and the mixture is smooth. Chill for 1 hour or until cool to the touch. Whip the mixture with the whisk attachment of an electric mixer until fluffy and swirl it on the top of the cake.

# "Birdseed" Cake

*When my sons Jay and Dan were small, they used to
love to eat the trimmings of this almond-flavored génoise.
For some reason, the crumbs reminded them of birdseed and
they always invited their friends in to share the "birdseed."
The mother of one of their playmates actually called
and asked if she could order the "Birdseed Cake." That's
how it got its name, and it was the cake that
launched my pastry-making career.*

[Serves 10 to 12]

1 recipe Almond Génoise
(page 73)

1½ cups Crème Ganache
(page 75)

6 tablespoons rum

3½ cups Buttercream (page 76)

4 tablespoons kirsch (cherry
brandy)

1 cup crushed Nougatine
(page 83) or 1 cup crushed
English Toffee (page 50)

½ cup confectioners' sugar,
sifted

To assemble, cut the *génoise* in half horizontally. Trim the edges and cut the cake in half lengthwise, for four equal rectangles. Melt ½ cup of the *ganache* and set aside. Place one cake rectangle on a platter and drizzle 2 tablespoons of rum on top. Mix 2 more tablespoons of rum with ¾ cup of the buttercream and spread on the cake. Place a layer of cake on top of the buttercream. Drizzle the remaining rum on top. Whip the remaining *ganache* until it lightens and holds its shape. Spread it on the cake layer and place the third cake layer on top. Drizzle 2 tablespoons of kirsch on top. Mix the remaining kirsch with another ¾ cup of buttercream and the crushed Nougatine or English Toffee and spread it on the layer. Top with the remaining layer of cake.

Mix the melted *ganache* with the remaining buttercream and spread it on the sides of the cake to cover. Dust the top with confectioners' sugar. Chill several hours or overnight. To serve, slice into ½-inch portions.

# Baked Apple Cake

*I've never seen a recipe for an apple cake quite like this one,*
*a homey, comforting dessert that makes a perfect finish for a*
*soup and salad meal. And it has a heavenly aroma!*

[Serves 6]

¾ cup dry white wine

Zest of one lemon

⅓ cup sugar

½ teaspoon ground cinnamon

3 tart apples (such as Granny
Smith), peeled, halved,
and cored

TOPPING

3 large eggs, separated

2 tablespoons sugar

½ cup heavy cream

1 tablespoon unsalted butter,
melted

½ cup all-purpose flour, sifted

½ teaspoon baking powder

1 cup whipped cream flavored
with calvados (apple brandy)

Preheat the oven to 375° F. Butter an 8 × 8 × 2-inch baking dish, preferably Pyrex. Set a shallow pan on the lowest shelf of the oven and fill it with water.

Place the wine, lemon zest, sugar, and cinnamon in a 4-quart pot and simmer for 5 minutes. Add the apples and poach them, covered, at medium heat until tender, about 15 minutes.

Arrange the apples cut side down in the baking dish and pour the cooking liquid over the apples. Set aside.

To make the topping, beat the egg yolks with 1 tablespoon of the sugar until thickened and light in color. Add the cream and butter. Sift the flour with the baking powder and add to the egg mixture.

In a separate bowl, beat the egg whites with the remaining 1 tablespoon sugar until stiff but not dry. Fold a little of the egg-yolk mixture into the whites, then fold the whites into the remaining yolk mixture and blend until there are no streaks of white. Pour the batter over the apples.

Set the baking dish on the middle shelf of the oven and bake the cake for approximately 25 minutes or until golden brown. Serve at room temperature with the whipped cream. This is best served the same day.

# Viennese Chocolate Fantasy

*This is my version of the famous Sacher Torte.*
*Raspberry jam can be substituted for the apricot preserves*
*for a different taste.*

[Serves 8 to 10]

10 ounces semisweet chocolate
   (Lindt Excellence works well)
1 tablespoon rum
½ cup light cream
½ cup (1 stick) unsalted butter,
   well chilled and cut into
   small pieces
5 large eggs, separated
⅓ cup sugar
½ cup cornstarch, sifted
6 ounces good-quality apricot
   preserves

GLAZE
8 ounces bittersweet chocolate
½ cup (1 stick) unsalted butter

Preheat the oven to 350° F. Butter and flour two 8-inch round cake pans.

In a medium metal mixing bowl, combine the chocolate, rum, and cream over hot, but not boiling, water, stirring frequently until melted. Remove from the heat and add the butter one piece at a time, beating with a whisk or hand-held electric mixer after each addition. In another metal bowl, beat the egg yolks and 1 tablespoon of the sugar until light and lemon-colored. Fold the egg-yolk mixture into the chocolate mixture and whisk together until smooth and fluffy. Immediately fold the cornstarch into the chocolate mixture and blend well.

In a separate bowl, beat the egg whites until they hold soft peaks, then gradually beat in the remaining sugar until the meringue is shiny. Fold one-quarter of the meringue into the chocolate mixture, then fold in the rest of the meringue until no streaks of white show.

Pour the batter into the prepared pans and bake for about 20 minutes or until a few crumbs cling to a toothpick inserted into the middle of the cake. Cool the cakes in the pans for about 10 minutes, then invert onto a rack. When completely cool, place one layer on a plate and cover the top with apricot preserves. Place the second layer, bottom side up, on top of the first layer.

To make the glaze, combine the chocolate and butter in a 1-quart saucepan and place over low heat until the chocolate is melted and the mixture is smooth. Let the glaze cool for a few minutes at room temperature, then pour about a third over the top of the cake, just to the edge. Cool the remaining chocolate further by refrigerating it for about 10 minutes, or by resting the pan in a bowl of ice water for a few minutes until the chocolate is at room temperature. Beat with a mixer until the glaze is thick and fluffy, then spread it around the sides of the cake. Serve the cake at room temperature in thin slices.

# Chocolate Raspberry Torte

*The flavors of chocolate and raspberry*
*make a choice combination. This is one of my most*
*often requested cakes.*

**[Serves 10 to 12]**

1 10-inch Chocolate Génoise (page 72)

2 tablespoons sugar

½ cup water

4 tablespoons framboise (raspberry brandy), the best you can afford

1 cup seedless red raspberry jam

3 cups Egg Yolk Buttercream (page 77)

½ pint fresh raspberries

3 cups Crème Ganache (page 75)

Cut the *génoise* horizontally into 3 equal layers. Place one layer on a serving platter. Combine the sugar, water, and 2 tablespoons of the framboise. Brush one-third of the mixture on the cake, then spread evenly with the raspberry jam. Mix the remaining framboise with 1 cup of the buttercream and spread evenly over the jam. Press the fresh raspberries into the buttercream and smooth the surface with a spatula. Place the second *génoise* layer on top and brush with another one-third of the framboise mixture.

Place 2 cups of the *ganache* in the bowl of an electric mixer, or use a portable hand-held mixer, and whip until fluffy and light in color. (If the *ganache* seems very firm and hard to spread, it can be warmed by placing the bowl in a container of hot water for a few seconds until it reaches the proper consistency.) Spread the *ganache* over the second layer. Place the third layer on top and brush with the remaining framboise mixture. In the same bowl used to whip the *ganache*, heat the remaining *ganache* very briefly, just until softened. Add the remaining 2 cups of buttercream. Whip with the whisk attachment of an electric mixer until fluffy and no streaks of chocolate show. Spread on the top and sides of the cake. Refrigerate for several hours.

If sliced very thin, this will make as many as 18 servings.

# Lemon Buttercream Torte

*This delicate, tart cake makes an elegant finish
for a company dinner. Decorate the top with
fresh raspberries, if you like.*

**[Serves 10 to 12]**

⅔ cup fresh lemon juice

1 cup water

¼ cup sugar

3 cups Egg Yolk Buttercream
(page 77)

1 recipe Lemon Cream Jean-
Louis (page 79)

1 10-inch Yellow Génoise
(page 71)

Combine ⅓ cup of the lemon juice with the water and sugar to make a syrup. Set aside. Combine the buttercream with ⅔ cup lemon cream and the remaining lemon juice. Mix well. (If the cream looks separated, heat it over a little hot water, stirring for about 30 seconds.) Set aside.

Using a serrated knife, slice the *génoise* horizontally into three layers. Place one layer on a cake plate and brush with the lemon syrup. Spread with a thin layer of buttercream, then ½ cup lemon cream. Spread a thin layer of buttercream on another layer of cake and place the layer, buttercream side down, on the first layer. Brush the top with the lemon syrup and spread with a thin layer of buttercream, then with ½ cup of lemon cream. Spread a thin layer of buttercream on the third layer of cake and place the layer, buttercream side down, on the second layer. Brush the top with the remaining lemon syrup and cover the top and sides of the cake with the remaining buttercream. Chill before serving.

**Note:** You can vary the cake by spreading on one layer only of fresh raspberries mixed with some raspberry jam instead of the lemon cream and buttercream.

# Amaretti Meringue Torte

*The Amaretti di Saronno cookies that flavor the meringue make all the difference in taste. The cookies are Lazzaroni brand, available in distinctive orange-and-red cans filled with delicately wrapped packages containing two cookies each.*

[Serves 8 to 10]

6 large egg whites

½ teaspoon cream of tartar

1 teaspoon vanilla extract

¾ cup granulated sugar

1 tablespoon cornstarch

14 Amaretti di Saronno cookies, crushed

8 ounces bittersweet chocolate, melted

3 cups heavy cream

1 tablespoon confectioners' sugar

3 tablespoons Amaretto di Saronno liqueur

½ pint fresh strawberries, wiped with a damp cloth, hulled, and sliced in half

Preheat the oven to 250° F. Line 2 baking sheets (at least 10 × 13 inches) with parchment paper.

Beat the egg whites with the cream of tartar and vanilla until white and foamy. Gradually add all except 1 tablespoon of the granulated sugar and continue beating until very stiff and shiny, about 5 minutes. Mix the cornstarch with the reserved granulated sugar and crushed cookies and fold into the meringue.

With a spatula, spread half the meringue onto baking sheet to form a 10-inch round about ½ inch thick. Repeat with the remaining meringue on the second sheet. Bake for ½ hour, rotating the trays for more even baking. Continue baking for 1 hour, or until the meringues are pale beige in color and feel dry and firm to the touch but are still pliable. They will become brittle and completely dry as they cool. (One way to ensure complete cooking is to turn off the oven and leave the meringues in overnight.) When done, the meringues will detach easily from the parchment.

Spread half the melted chocolate in a thin layer on top of one round. Spread the remaining chocolate in a thin layer on the smooth bottom side of the second round. While the chocolate is hardening, whip the cream with the confectioners' sugar until stiff peaks form. Add the Amaretto di Saronno and combine well. Add the strawberries to half of the whipped cream and spread on top of the first meringue round. Place the second round, chocolate side up, on top. Cover the sides of the torte with the remaining whipped cream. This can be served immediately or refrigerated for several hours.

To serve, cut into wedges with a sharp, serrated knife, using a gentle sawing motion to slice through the top layer. Once you've cut through the first layer, the knife will move easily through the whipped cream, and the bottom layer can be cut by forcing the knife down hard through the meringue without using the sawing motion. Or, before assembling the torte, you can slice the top layer separately, then place the wedges close together on top of the filled bottom layer.

# Caramel Nut Torte

*This cake was a favorite of diners at
Jean-Louis at the Watergate.*

[Serves 12 to 14]

1 cup raisins

1 cup walnuts, chopped

¼ cup plus 2 tablespoons dark
rum

2 tablespoons sugar

½ cup water

1 double recipe Caramel Sauce
(page 82), room temperature

8 ounces (2 sticks) unsalted
butter, room temperature

1 recipe Yellow Génoise (page
71), for a 10-inch cake

1 cup Crème Ganache (page 75)

Place the raisins and walnuts in a small bowl
with ¼ cup of rum. Set aside.

Dissolve the sugar in the water. Add the
remaining 2 tablespoons of rum and set
aside.

Place the caramel sauce in the bowl of an
electric mixer and beat with the whisk attachment at medium speed for about 2 minutes.
The sauce should lighten and thicken somewhat. Add the butter by tablespoonfuls, continuing to beat the mixture until it has the
consistency of buttercream. (If the mixture
looks separated, heat it over a little hot water
and whip for 1 minute more.) Set aside.

Using a serrated knife, slice the cake horizontally into 2 layers. Place
one layer on a cake plate and brush with half of the rum syrup. Spread ½
cup of the caramel buttercream on top and distribute the raisins and
walnuts evenly over the cream, pressing them into the buttercream. Spread
1 cup of the caramel buttercream over the raisins and walnuts and add the
second cake layer. Brush the remaining rum syrup on top. With a metal
spatula cover the cake with the remaining caramel buttercream. Chill for
several hours or overnight.

Several hours before serving, melt the ganache over hot water and pour
over the top of the torte, letting it drizzle down the sides. Chill for at least
one hour.

# Pies

### *and*

# Tarts

*Blueberry Sour Cream Pie*

*Toasted Coconut Pecan Pie*

*Cheese Danish Pie*

*Turtle Pie*

*Very Crisp Apple Tart*

*Orange Frangipane Tart*

*Baked Lemon Tart*

*Amaretto Nougat Tart*

# Blueberry Sour Cream Pie

*When I worked at The Big Cheese restaurant in
Georgetown, this was one of the most requested desserts.
It is simple to make, and even easier if you use
a graham-cracker crust.*

[Serves 8 to 10]

1 Sweet Dough Pastry 9-inch
pie shell (page 74),
prebaked

1 12-ounce jar red currant
jelly

1½ pints fresh blueberries

2 cups sour cream

2 tablespoons brown sugar

1 teaspoon ground cinnamon

Preheat the oven to 350° F. Have the pie shell
ready.

Place the jelly in a small saucepan and
bring to a boil over high heat. Lower the heat
to medium and cook for 3 minutes, until
the jelly is completely melted and slightly
thickened.

Rinse and drain the berries in a colander.
Pick them over to remove any stems or small
leaves, then place them in the pie shell. Pour
the jelly over the berries. Combine the sour cream, brown sugar, and
cinnamon and spoon over the berries.

Bake for 5 minutes. Cool on a wire rack. Chill for at least 2 hours before
serving.

# Toasted Coconut Pecan Pie

*Coconut adds an interesting flavor and texture
to this popular pie.*

[Serves 8 to 10]

1 recipe Sweet Dough Pastry
(page 74), for 1 10-inch
pie shell

1½ cups brown sugar

4 large eggs

2 teaspoons fresh lemon juice

1 teaspoon vanilla extract

½ cup (1 stick) unsalted butter,
melted

3 cups pecan halves

2 cups shredded coconut,
preferably unsweetened

Preheat the oven to 350° F.

Line the pie shell with aluminum foil and fill with dried beans or rice. Bake for 15 minutes, then remove the foil and beans. Bake 5 minutes more or until the bottom of the crust is light brown and firm. Set aside.

Place the brown sugar, eggs, lemon juice, and vanilla in a medium bowl and stir until well combined and smooth. Add the butter and mix well. Stir in the pecans and coconut.

Pour into the pie shell and bake for approximately 45 minutes or until the filling is set and browned. If the top becomes too brown while baking, cover it with a piece of aluminum foil. Let the pie cool on a wire rack. Serve warm or at room temperature.

# Cheese Danish Pie

*I love cheese danish, and what better way
to have enough of my favorite part, the filling,
than to bake it in a pie.*

[Serves 8 to 10]

1 cup white raisins

4 tablespoons Grand Marnier

1 recipe Sweet Dough Pastry
(page 74) for 1 9-inch pie
shell

16 ounces (1 pound) cream
cheese, room temperature

1 tablespoon unsalted butter,
room temperature

4 tablespoons dry curd cottage
cheese

2 tablespoons sour cream

½ cup sugar

1 large egg

3 tablespoons flour

1 teaspoon vanilla extract

Grated zest of one lemon

Preheat the oven to 350° F.

Soak the raisins and Grand Marnier in a
medium bowl. Set aside.

Line the pie shell with aluminum foil and
fill with dried beans or rice. Bake for 15 minutes, then remove the foil and beans. Bake 5
minutes more or until the bottom of the crust
is light brown and firm. Set aside.

Place the cream cheese, butter, cottage
cheese, and sour cream in the bowl of an
electric mixer and beat at medium speed for 1
minute with the paddle attachment. Add the
sugar and the egg and beat at medium speed
for one minute. Add the flour and vanilla and
mix well with a rubber spatula, scraping the
bottom and sides of the bowl. Add the lemon
zest and raisins and combine well. Pour the
mixture into the pie shell and bake at 350° F
for about 40 minutes or until the top is firm and browned around the edges.
If the crust begins to brown too quickly, cover with strips of aluminum foil.
A cake tester inserted in the middle of the pie should come out clean. Cool
the pie on a rack, then chill for several hours before serving.

# Turtle Pie

*A mile-high creation made with milk chocolate,
nuts, and caramel—all the flavors of a favorite candy bar.
This is a rich dessert and a little goes a long way.*

[Serves 8 to 10]

1 recipe Sweet Dough Pastry (page 74), prebaked in a 9-inch pie plate

16 ounces (1 pound) milk chocolate, chopped into 1-inch pieces

3 cups heavy cream, chilled

1 cup unsalted cashews, finely chopped

3 strips Creamy Caramels (page 49), cut into slices ¼ inch wide

2 teaspoons confectioners' sugar

1 teaspoon vanilla extract

Cocoa powder

Place the chocolate in a medium-sized metal bowl and place over a *bain-marie* of hot, but not boiling, water. Stir frequently until melted and smooth.

Whip 2 cups of the cream until soft peaks form. Fold the cream into the warm chocolate with a rubber spatula until no streaks show. Gently fold in the nuts and caramels. Pour the mixture into the pie shell, smoothing the top with a thin-bladed metal spatula.

Chill for four hours or overnight. Several hours before serving, whip the remaining cream with the sugar and vanilla until firm peaks form. Swirl the cream over the top of the pie and decorate with a dusting of cocoa.

# Very Crisp Apple Tart

*This classic apple tart retains the fresh flavor
of the apples by being filled just before serving. A quick run
under the broiler softens the sliced apples while
keeping the crust crisp and dry.*

[Serves 8]

1 recipe Sweet Dough Pastry
(page 74), prebaked in a
9-inch tart shell

APPLE MARMALADE
8 McIntosh apples
6 ounces apricot jam
Zest of 1 orange
2 teaspoons vanilla extract

TOPPING
3 large Granny Smith apples
Juice of 1 lemon (optional)
1 cup Apricot Glaze (page 81),
warmed

To make the marmalade, peel and core the McIntosh apples and chop into medium-sized chunks. Place the apple chunks in a heavy 3-quart pot, cover, and cook over low heat for about 15 minutes, stirring often. When the apples have softened and can be broken with a spoon, add the apricot jam. Cook, uncovered, over medium-high heat for about 8 minutes, stirring frequently. When done, the apples will have lost a lot of moisture and will form a mound on a spoon. Remove from the heat and stir in the orange zest and vanilla. Set aside.

Peel and core the Granny Smith apples, cut them in half, and thinly slice across the broad side of the apple. If the apples are not being used right away, sprinkle the lemon juice over the slices to prevent them from turning brown. Just before serving, pour the apple marmalade into the tart shell. Cover with the apple slices in overlapping concentric circles. (On occasion, I have microwaved the apple slices separately for about 3 minutes at the highest power to soften them before placing them on the tart.) Run under the broiler for about 3 minutes or until the apples have browned slightly. Brush the top with warm Apricot Glaze. Serve warm.

# Orange Frangipane Tart

*Orange flower water, which flavors this tart,
has an exotic scent that reminds me of springtime.
It's available in gourmet shops or in the
gourmet section of the supermarket.*

[Serves 8 to 10]

1 recipe Sweet Dough Pastry (page 74), partially baked in a 10-inch tart shell

2 cups or 2 8-ounce cans almond paste

3 large eggs

½ cup confectioners' sugar

½ cup (1 stick) unsalted butter

5 to 6 large navel oranges

2 tablespoons orange flower water

Apricot Glaze (page 81)

Preheat the oven to 350° F. Have the tart shell ready.

Break the almond paste into large chunks and place in the bowl of an electric mixer. Add the eggs, confectioners' sugar, and butter and beat with the paddle attachment until well combined. Finely grate the zest of one orange and stir into the butter mixture. Stir in the orange flower water and pour the mixture into the tart shell. Bake on the middle rack of the oven for about 20 minutes, until the edges are brown and the top is golden and firm. Cool on a wire rack.

Meanwhile, peel the remaining oranges and separate into sections, removing any white pith and the membrane. Arrange the orange sections on the tart in overlapping concentric circles, covering the entire surface of the tart. Brush with warmed Apricot Glaze. This is best served at room temperature.

# Baked Lemon Tart

*This intensely lemon-flavored custard
baked in a sweet tart shell makes a simple yet elegant
end to a special dinner.*

[Serves 8]

1 recipe Sweet Dough Pastry
(page 74), prebaked in an
8-inch tart mold

3 large eggs

½ cup fresh lemon juice

¾ cup sugar

⅔ cup heavy cream

Preheat the oven to 325° F. Have the tart shell ready. Place the remaining ingredients in a medium bowl and mix with a wire whisk until well combined and frothy.

Fill the tart shell half full with the mixture. Place on the middle rack of the oven. Using a ladle, add the remaining mixture to the shell until it reaches the top of the mold.

Bake for approximately 20 minutes. The tart should shimmer in the center and seem slightly underdone. Cool on a rack for 15 minutes. Unmold and chill for several hours before serving. This is best eaten the same day.

# Amaretto Nougat Tart

*You'll find that this tart is very easy to put
together if you have some of the basic ingredients
on hand. Try it as a special finish to a
light summer lunch or dinner.*

[Serves 8 to 10]

1 10-inch layer Yellow Génoise
(page 71)
1 recipe Sweet Dough Pastry
(page 74), prebaked in a
10-inch tart shell
4 tablespoons Amaretto di
Saronno liqueur
3 cups heavy cream
1 cup coarsely crushed
Nougatine (page 83)
½ cup finely chopped bittersweet
chocolate

Using a serrated knife, slice the *génoise* horizontally into 3 even layers. Place one layer in the baked tart shell. (Tightly wrap and freeze the remaining layers for another use.) Brush the top of the layer with 2 tablespoons of the Amaretto.

Whip the cream until stiff. Place the cream in a large bowl and add the Nougatine, chocolate, and remaining Amaretto. Fold gently until well combined. Pour the mixture into the tart shell carefully, smoothing the top with a metal spatula.

Chill for at least 2 hours before serving.

# Cookies
*and*
# Candies

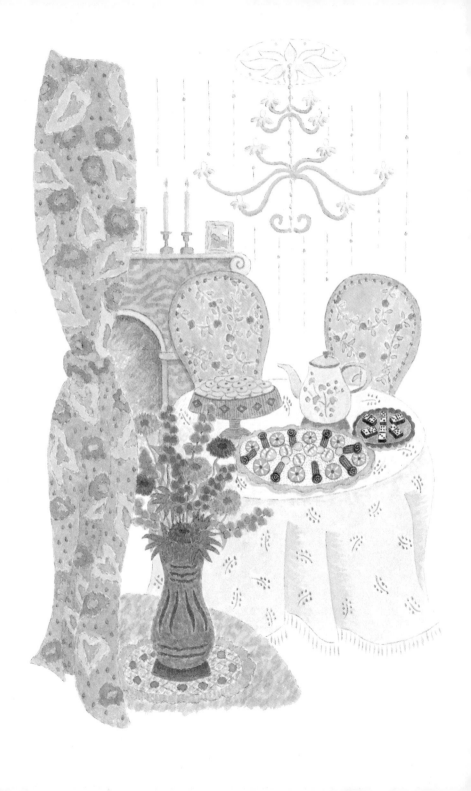

*Almond Lace Cookies*

*Vanilla Butter Buttons*

*Palets aux Raisins*

*Miniature Gingersnaps*

*Walnut Snowballs*

*Gâteaux Bretonnes*

*Chocolate Truffle Cookies*

*Maryland Strudel*

*Macaroon Logs*

*White Chocolate Truffles*

*Creamy Caramels*

*English Toffee*

# Almond Lace Cookies

*These tender, lacy cookies are lovely for afternoon tea.*
*They are best made on a cool, dry day.*

[Makes 25 cookies]

⅔ cup blanched almonds, finely chopped

½ cup sugar

½ cup unsalted butter

3 teaspoons all-purpose flour

2 tablespoons light cream

Preheat the oven to 350° F. Line 3 cookie sheets with parchment.

Combine all the ingredients in a heavy 2-quart saucepan and place over low heat. Stir until the butter melts. Continue cooking until the mixture is bubbly and pulls away from the sides of the pan.

Drop teaspoonfuls of dough 1 inch apart on the cookie sheets. Bake one sheet at a time on the middle rack of the oven for 6 to 8 minutes, until the cookies are light brown. Let cool for about 1 minute, then remove the cookies from the sheets with a very thin-bladed spatula. Handle carefully since they break quite easily. They can be stored in an airtight tin for several days.

**Note:** If you work quickly when removing the warm cookies from the cookie sheets, you can curve each around a clean broom handle and, when cool, fill with sweetened, flavored whipped cream.

# Vanilla Butter Buttons

*These cookies are irresistible. No bigger*
*than one bite, they melt in the mouth. They are best*
*made in cool, dry weather.*

[Makes 125 tiny cookies]

¾ cup (1½ sticks) unsalted
    butter
⅓ cup sugar
1 large egg
1 teaspoon vanilla extract
¾ cup all-purpose flour

Preheat the oven to 350° F. Have ready a pastry bag fitted with a ½-inch tip. Line 3 baking sheets with parchment.

Using an electric mixer with a paddle attachment, cream the butter and sugar together on the lowest speed until pale and fluffy. Still on the lowest speed, add the egg and vanilla, then gradually add the flour. When the dough becomes too stiff to stir by machine, mix in any remaining flour by hand.

Fill the pastry bag half full and pipe ¼-inch balls of dough 1 inch apart on the cookie sheets. Bake one tray at a time on the middle rack of the oven, turning the trays after 5 minutes. Bake 5 minutes more, or until the cookies are brown on the edges and set in the center. Watch carefully since these cookies brown quickly. Let cool before removing from the sheets. Store in the refrigerator in airtight tins.

# Palets aux Raisins

*The apricot-rum glaze gives this cookie a festive
appearance and an unusual taste.*

[Makes 60 cookies]

½ cup (1 stick) unsalted butter
¾ cup confectioners' sugar
1 large egg
1 teaspoon vanilla extract
1⅓ cups cake flour, sifted
1 cup currants
1 12-ounce jar apricot jam,
  strained through a sieve
¾ cup confectioners' sugar
  mixed with 2 tablespoons
  dark rum

Preheat the oven to 350° F. Line 2 baking sheets with parchment. Have ready a pastry bag fitted with a ¾-inch plain tip.

Place the butter and the ¾ cup confectioners' sugar in the bowl of an electric mixer. Using the paddle attachment, cream at low speed until the mixture is fluffy and light in color. Add the egg and vanilla, mixing just until combined. With a rubber spatula, slowly fold in the flour, one-third at a time. Add the currants and mix them evenly through the dough.

Fill the pastry bag two-thirds full and pipe 1-inch mounds of dough about 2 inches apart on the baking sheets. Bake approximately 10 to 12 minutes, until the edges of the cookies are golden brown and the centers are set.

While the cookies are baking, bring the apricot jam to a boil, then let it sit over low heat to keep it fluid until ready to use. As soon as the cookies are removed from the oven, brush with the jam and then quickly brush on the rum sugar. The melting sugar will form a lustrous coating.

The cookies can be kept covered in the refrigerator, but the glaze may turn dull. They are best eaten the same day they're baked.

# Miniature Gingersnaps

*These tiny cookies are perfect for a tea platter.*
*Serve them with Vanilla Butter Buttons (page 40) and Chocolate*
*Truffle Cookies (page 45) for a delicious assortment.*

[Makes 100 one-inch cookies]

¾ cup (1½ sticks) unsalted
butter

1 cup dark brown sugar, firmly
packed

¼ cup molasses

1 large egg

2 cups all-purpose flour

1 teaspoon baking soda

1½ teaspoons ground cinnamon

½ teaspoon ground cloves

2 teaspoons ground ginger

Preheat the oven to 350° F. Line 3 baking sheets with parchment. Have ready a pastry bag with a plain ½-inch tip.

Place the butter and brown sugar in the bowl of an electric mixer and cream on the lowest speed with the paddle attachment. Add the molasses and egg and mix just until combined. Sift together the flour, baking soda, and spices. Add to the butter mixture and blend well with a rubber spatula.

Fill the pastry bag two-thirds full and pipe ½-inch mounds of dough 2 inches apart on the baking sheets. Bake 10 to 12 minutes or until the cookies feel dry and firm on top. Cool for 10 minutes on baking sheets.

This will make a very chewy cookie; if you prefer crisp cookies, you can bake them a bit longer. The cookies will keep for several weeks stored in an airtight container in the refrigerator.

# Walnut Snowballs

*When my friend Lincoln Mudd, in his role as recipe*
*taster, tried these, he immediately exclaimed "Snowballs!"*
*He remembered having these meltingly soft cookies as a child.*
*There is no egg in this recipe, resulting in a delicate*
*cookie with a crumbly texture.*

**[Makes 45 cookies]**

1 cup (2 sticks) unsalted butter
2⅓ cups confectioners' sugar
1 teaspoon vanilla extract
1 cup walnuts, finely chopped
½ teaspoon baking powder
2¼ cups all-purpose flour

Preheat the oven to 350° F. Line 2 baking sheets with parchment.

Place the butter and ⅓ cup of the confectioners' sugar in the bowl of an electric mixer and cream on low speed with the paddle attachment. Stir in the vanilla and walnuts with a rubber spatula.

Sift together the baking powder and flour. Add in thirds to the butter mixture, mixing with a rubber spatula after each addition. Form the dough into small walnut-size balls and place 1-inch apart on the baking sheets.

Bake about 15 minutes, until the cookies are set but not colored. Cool slightly. Before removing the cookies from the baking sheets, sift the remaining confectioners' sugar over them to cover completely. Store in an airtight container in the refrigerator.

# Gâteaux Bretonnes

*When I was a child, I tasted a very thin, waferlike
cookie at a country store in Maryland. I have never since
tasted anything similar except for this thin and delicate
cookie sandwich. The recipe takes a little
extra time to prepare, but it makes an extremely
elegant and sophisticated dessert.*

[Makes 16 to 18 thin gâteaux]

½ cup (1 stick) unsalted butter

⅓ cup sugar

3 large egg yolks

1 cup all-purpose flour, sifted

Zest of 1 lemon, grated

Apricot Cream (page 80), or

Lemon Cream Jean-Louis

(page 79)

½ pint raspberries or other

berries for decoration

Preheat the oven to 325° F. Have ready a pastry bag with a ½-inch tip. Line 3 baking sheets with parchment.

Place the butter and sugar in an electric mixer and cream on low speed using the paddle attachment. Add the egg yolks and mix just until combined. With a rubber spatula, fold in the flour and then the lemon zest.

Fill the pastry bag two-thirds full and pipe 1½-inch mounds of the paste 4 inches apart on the baking sheets. Using a small offset spatula, spread the paste out in circles as thinly as possible, perhaps ⅛ inch.

Bake approximately 10 to 12 minutes, watching the cookies carefully. When done, they should be lightly colored and golden brown around the edges. While the cookies are still warm, run a thin-bladed spatula under each to loosen it from the parchment. Let cool on the baking sheets. At this point the cookies can be stacked in fours, wrapped in plastic wrap, and refrigerated or frozen.

Just before serving, spread half of the cookies with a thin, smooth layer of Apricot Cream or Lemon Cream Jean-Louis and top with a second cookie. Arrange on separate dessert plates, decorate with a few berries, and serve immediately.

# Chocolate Truffle Cookies

*These cookies freeze so beautifully, it's worthwhile making a large batch.*

[Makes 150 very tiny cookies]

1 cup (2 sticks) unsalted butter
1 cup sugar
1 large egg and 1 large egg yolk
1 teaspoon vanilla extract
2 ounces unsweetened chocolate, melted and cooled to room temperature
1½ cups all-purpose flour, sifted with ¼ cup Dutch processed cocoa powder
½ teaspoon baking powder
2 cups Crème Ganache (page 75)

Preheat the oven to 350° F. Line 4 baking sheets with parchment. Have ready a pastry bag fitted with a ½-inch star tip. I use the Ateco #3 tip for this recipe.

Place the butter and sugar in the bowl of an electric mixer and cream together on the lowest speed, using the paddle attachment. Still on the lowest speed, mix in the egg, yolk, and vanilla. Add the chocolate and mix by hand to combine well. Sift together the flour-cocoa mixture and baking powder. Add to the creamed mixture one-quarter at a time, blending well with a rubber spatula after each addition.

Fill the pastry bag two-thirds full and pipe out 1-inch strips of dough onto the baking sheets. Bake for 10 minutes or until the cookies feel firm to the touch. Let cool on wire racks. (At this point the cookies can be tightly wrapped and frozen until ready to use.)

Fit a clean pastry bag with a ½-inch star tip and decorate the cookies by piping a rosette of whipped *ganache* (see whipping directions in recipe on page 18) at the tip of each cookie strip. The *ganache* will harden after a moment, making the cookies stackable on trays. Chill for 1 hour before serving.

# Maryland Strudel

*Many people tell me that this strudel reminds
them of pastry that their grandmothers made. The low
oven temperature and slow baking produce a
delicate color and flaky crust.*

**[Makes 40 one-inch slices]**

1 cup (2 sticks) unsalted
butter, melted

1 cup sour cream

1 tablespoon sugar

2 cups all-purpose flour, sifted

FILLING

24 ounces apricot preserves,
processed until smooth in a
blender or food processor

1 box (15 ounces) white
raisins

1 box (15 ounces) dark raisins

1½ pounds walnuts, finely
chopped

4 teaspoons ground cinnamon

Preheat the oven to 325° F. Line 2 cookie sheets with a double thickness of parchment paper.

Combine the butter, sour cream, and sugar and mix until well blended. Add the flour and mix just until blended. The dough will look mealy. Gather the dough into a ball and wrap in plastic wrap. Refrigerate for 3 hours or overnight.

Divide the dough into 4 equal parts. Work with one piece of dough at a time, keeping the rest refrigerated. Place the dough on a well-floured surface, knead it briefly, then roll it out into a rectangle approximately 8 × 12 inches. The dough should be thin enough so that you can almost see through it. Keep the surface floured to prevent the dough from sticking.

Spread one-quarter of the apricot preserves over the dough, leaving a ½-inch border all around. Sprinkle one-quarter of the raisins and walnuts over the preserves and dust with 1 teaspoon of cinnamon. Fold the sides of the dough over the filling, then roll the dough lengthwise, jelly-roll fashion, ending with the seam on the bottom. Quickly lift the roll and place it, seam side down, onto the baking sheet. Repeat the process with the remaining dough. Chill the rolls for about 15 minutes before baking.

Bake for 45 minutes to 1 hour, or until light golden. While still warm, cut each roll into 10 slices with a serrated knife. The strudel will keep for at least a week in the refrigerator, or it can be frozen.

# Macaroon Logs

*Macaroon lovers will find these the easiest to make. Their unusual shape makes them a nice addition to the cookie platter.*

**[Makes about 16 two-inch cookies]**

1 8-ounce can almond paste
⅓ cup confectioners' sugar
1 large egg white
Grated zest of 1 orange

Preheat the oven to 350° F. Line a baking sheet with parchment.

Break the almond paste into rough chunks directly into the bowl of an electric mixer. Add the remaining ingredients and beat with the paddle attachment until smooth.

Pinch off walnut-size pieces of the dough and roll each piece into a log shape approximately 2 inches long. Place the logs on the baking sheet and pinch the sides of each together to form a pyramid shape at the top. Bake for 15 minutes or until lightly colored. Cool on wire racks.

These cookies will keep for several weeks stored in an airtight container in the refrigerator.

# White Chocolate Truffles

*These bonbons are simple to make and always get raves.*

[Makes about 40 pieces]

1 pound good-quality white
chocolate (Lindt, Callebaut,
or Valrhona)

½ cup heavy cream

2 tablespoons Grand Marnier, or
liqueur of choice

Line a cookie sheet with parchment. Have ready a pastry bag fitted with a ½-inch plain pastry tip.

Chop half of the chocolate into ½-inch chunks. Reserve the rest. Place the cream in a 2-quart stainless-steel, heavy-bottomed pan. Bring to boil over high heat. Remove from heat and add chopped chocolate, stirring until melted and well combined. Chill for about ½ hour or until cool to the touch.

Place the chocolate mixture and the liqueur in the bowl of an electric mixer and whip with the whisk attachment until firm peaks form. (If the mixture is crumbly, it is probably too cold and needs to be dipped into a *bain-marie* of hot water for a few seconds. Whip again until the cream is smooth and has the consistency of whipped cream.)

Fill the pastry bag half full and pipe ½-inch balls of the mixture onto the cookie sheet, placing them as close together as possible without touching. Chill for a few hours or overnight.

Line a cookie sheet with parchment. Chop the remaining chocolate into ¼-inch chunks and place in a metal mixing bowl. Place the bowl in a *bain-marie* of hot water and stir the chocolate constantly with a rubber spatula until it is almost melted. Remove the bowl from the water and continue stirring until no chunks of chocolate remain. The bowl should feel tepid (if hotter, the chocolate will soften the truffle mixture; if colder, the chocolate will harden too quickly). Using a fork, dip the formed truffles one at a time in the bowl of melted chocolate, turning the fork to ensure even coverage, and quickly place each truffle on the parchment-lined sheet. Refrigerate until ready to serve, or freeze for up to 3 weeks.

# Creamy Caramels

*This is one of my most often requested recipes
and one of my own favorite candies.*

[Makes 60 pieces]

2 cups plus 2 tablespoons heavy cream

2½ cups sugar

2 tablespoons clear corn syrup

2 teaspoons vanilla extract

4 tablespoons (½ stick) unsalted butter

Thinly coat the sides and bottom of an 8 × 8-inch rectangular baking pan with vegetable oil. (One with squared rather than rounded edges is preferable.) Set aside.

Place the cream, sugar, corn syrup, and vanilla in a 1-quart heavy-bottomed pot and stir until the sugar and cream are combined. Wash down the sides of the pot with a pastry brush dipped in cold water, making sure no sugar crystals remain. Place the pot over high heat and stir until the sugar has dissolved and comes to a boil, about 2 minutes. Wash down the sides of the pot since the sugar mixture will rise up rather high in the pot as it starts to boil, then recede. Lower the heat and cook until the caramel is the color of brown wrapping paper and a candy thermometer registers 255° F. Remove from the heat and immediately add the butter, stirring until melted and the mixture is smooth. If it seems a little curdled, you haven't stirred enough. Keep stirring and the mixture will smooth out and become silken. Pour into the prepared pan and refrigerate overnight to harden.

To cut into the caramels, cut a 1-inch-wide strip down the length of the pan. Remove the strip and cut into squares. Using a thin-bladed pancake flipper, lift the remaining sheet of caramel from the pan and cut into strips and then into squares. The caramels should be stored in the refrigerator, wrapped in plastic wrap. If they are left at room temperature, the sugar will crystalize and the candy will become somewhat gritty—although some people prefer it that way!

# English Toffee

*This is one of my oldest recipes and one I
always come back to. The tang and crunch of the candy
really enlivens so many desserts, from the "Birdseed" Cake
(page 14) to the Chocolate Bombe (page 64).*

[Makes 3 pounds]

3 cups chopped hazelnuts

3 cups sugar

½ cup water

⅓ cup light corn syrup

2 teaspoons vanilla extract

2 cups (4 sticks) unsalted butter

Preheat the oven to 175° F. Coat a cookie tray—any baking tray with sides—with vegetable oil and set aside. Place the hazelnuts in an 8-inch cake pan and warm in the oven until ready to use.

Place the sugar, water, corn syrup, and vanilla in a 6-quart heavy-bottomed saucepan and stir well to dissolve the sugar. Wash down the sides of the pan with a pastry brush dipped in cold water, making sure no sugar crystals remain. Cook the mixture over high heat until it reaches a boil, stirring often and washing the sides of the pot with the brush dipped in cold water. Let the mixture boil for 1 minute. Add the butter, stirring to combine. Wash down the sides of the pan one last time and continue to boil, stirring often. Make sure to scrape the bottom of the pan to keep the mixture from burning. The mixture will be done when it registers 290° F. on a candy thermometer and is the color of a brown paper bag. Remove from the heat and stir in the hazelnuts.

Turn the mixture out onto the oiled sheet and let it cool completely. Break the toffee into pieces and wrap in plastic wrap. It will keep for several weeks at room temperature if wrapped in plastic and stored in an airtight container.

# Cold
# Desserts

*Apple Lime Mousse*

*Lime Bavarian*

*Banana Mousse*

*Whiskey Mousse*

*Chocolate Brick*

*Triple Chocolate Terrine*

*Caramel Trifle*

*Pears Praline*

*Chocolate Bombe*

*Red and White Parfait*

# Apple Lime Mousse

*Many years ago, I came across a recipe using
canned applesauce and lime Jell-O. The result was such an
interesting meld of flavors that I decided to create a
recipe that would replicate the taste with fresh
ingredients. And here it is, a simple, light,
and tart summer dessert.*

[Serves 8 to 10]

1 envelope unflavored gelatin

¼ cup cold water

1 recipe Apple Marmalade
(page 31), with the orange
zest replaced with the zest of
2 limes

¾ cup fresh lime juice (about 5
medium limes)

1 teaspoon vanilla extract

1 cup sugar

2 cups heavy cream

In a small metal bowl, soften the gelatin in the cold water for 5 minutes or until spongy. Meanwhile, place the marmalade, lime juice, vanilla, and sugar in a 2-quart saucepan and stir over medium heat just until warmed. Place the bowl of gelatin in a *bain-marie* of hot water and stir until the gelatin is completely dissolved. Add to the apple mixture, pour into a medium nonreactive bowl, and stir well to combine thoroughly. Chill in the refrigerator for a few minutes, stirring occasionally, until the mixture is cool. You can hasten the chilling by placing the bowl in a larger bowl filled with ice water and stirring well.

Whip the cream until soft peaks form. Fold into the apple mixture and blend well. Spoon into individual ¾-cup dessert or soufflé cups or an 8-cup soufflé mold. Chill for several hours or overnight.

**Note:** To serve as a pie, spoon the mousse into a 10-inch graham cracker crust and chill as above.

# Lime Bavarian

*I can't think of anything more refreshing than the
flavor of lime in a summer dessert. I call this a bavarian
but it's actually a mousse. No matter what
you call it, you'll enjoy it.*

[Serves 10]

1 10-inch layer Yellow Génoise
(page 71)

1⅓ cups plus 2 tablespoons
sugar

Grated zest of 4 large limes

1¾ cups fresh lime juice (about
10 large limes)

8 large egg yolks

1 envelope plus 1½ teaspoons
powdered gelatin

2 cups heavy cream

6 large egg whites

Slice the *génoise* horizontally into 3 layers. Place one layer in the bottom of a 10-inch springform pan. (Tightly wrap and freeze the remaining layers for another use.)

Combine 2 tablespoons of the sugar, 1 tablespoon of the lime juice, and 4 tablespoons of water. Brush the *génoise* layer with the mixture. Whisk together the egg yolks, the zest, ⅔ cup of the sugar, and the remaining lime juice in a 3-quart stainless-steel mixing bowl. Place the bowl over simmering water and continue whisking until the mixture is thick and foamy and coats the back of a wooden spoon. Remove from the heat.

Soften the gelatin in ¼ cup of cold water. When the gelatin is spongy, after about 5 minutes, stir over hot water until dissolved and clear. Add to the lime mixture and stir well. Refrigerate, stirring often with a rubber spatula. (A cold *bain-marie* will hasten the chilling.)

When the mixture has cooled, beat the cream until soft peaks form. Whip the egg whites until light and foamy. Gradually add the remaining sugar, continuing to beat until the meringue is shiny and stiff. Using a rubber spatula, fold about half of the cream into the egg whites, combine well, and fold the egg-white mixture into the rest of the cream, combining well. Fold the egg white–cream mixture into the lime mixture, being sure to scrape the bottom of the bowl to combine thoroughly. Pour into the springform and chill at least 6 hours or overnight.

To unmold, run a thin-bladed knife along the inside of the mold, then loosen the sides of the springform. The bavarian can be served from the bottom of the springform, or transfer it to a platter by sliding a metal spatula under the cake layer and lifting carefully.

**Note:** I sometimes glaze the top with a thin layer of Lemon Cream Jean-Louis (page 79) just before serving.

# Banana Mousse

*This is a lightened variation of my childhood favorite,*
*banana cream pie.*

[Serves 8]

1 10-inch layer Yellow Génoise (page 71)

½ cup plus 1 tablespoon sugar

3 tablespoons dark rum

5 large egg yolks

1 generous cup dry white wine

1 envelope plus 1 teaspoon unflavored gelatin

2 cups heavy cream

2 medium bananas, very ripe

Juice of 1 lemon

TOPPING

3 large firm bananas

Juice of 1 lemon

1 cup Apricot Glaze (page 81)

Slice the *génoise* horizontally into 3 layers. Place one layer in a 10-inch springform pan. (Tightly wrap and freeze the remaining layers for another use.) Dissolve 1 tablespoon of sugar in 1 tablespoon of the rum mixed with ¼ cup water. Brush the mixture on the cake.

In a heavy, nonreactive 2-quart saucepan, combine the egg yolks, wine, and remaining sugar. Whisk over medium-high heat until thick and foamy, about 5 minutes. Set aside.

In a small metal bowl, mix the remaining rum with 2 tablespoons of cold water and add the gelatin. When the gelatin becomes spongy, after about 5 minutes, stir over hot water until dissolved. Stir into the wine mixture, place in a stainless-steel bowl, and chill in the refrigerator, stirring occasionally, until cool to the touch. You can hasten the cooling process with an ice-water *bain-marie*.

Whip the cream until firm peaks form. Purée the bananas with the lemon juice until smooth. Fold the whipped cream and bananas into the cooled wine mixture and mix gently until well combined. Pour into the springform pan and chill for several hours or overnight.

Just before serving, thinly slice 3 large bananas and sprinkle with the lemon juice. Run a thin-bladed knife around the sides of the springform to release the spring and remove the sides of the pan. Arrange overlapping banana slices on the top of the mousse. Brush with warmed Apricot Glaze.

# Whiskey Mousse

*My friend Patrick Musel, who is a fine pastry chef,*
*told me about a whiskey mousse he had made at a restaurant*
*where he worked. I liked the sound of it and*
*developed this recipe.*

**[Serves 10]**

2 cups milk

6 large egg yolks

1⅓ cups sugar

¼ cup water

4 large egg whites

2 cups heavy cream

½ cup bourbon whiskey

Raspberry Coulis (page 80), or fresh raspberries

Place the milk in a heavy, nonreactive 2-quart saucepan and bring to a boil over medium-high heat. In a medium bowl, beat the egg yolks with ⅓ cup of the sugar until very thick and light in color. Gradually pour 1 cup of the hot milk into the yolks, whisking as you pour. Return the mixture to the saucepan and stir over low heat until thick enough to coat a wooden spoon. Remove from the heat and whisk to cool. Refrigerate until ready to use.

Place the remaining sugar and the water in a small saucepan. Stir to dissolve the sugar, washing down the sides of the pan with a pastry brush dipped in cold water. Place the egg whites in the bowl of an electric mixer and beat on low speed. Meanwhile, cook the sugar syrup over high heat. When the syrup starts to boil, continue beating the egg whites at medium speed. Cook the syrup until a candy thermometer registers 242° F. or until a few drops of syrup form a firm ball when placed in cold water. Slowly pour the syrup into the egg whites, continuously beating on medium-high speed, until the mixture is cool. Whip the cream until soft peaks form. Set aside. Add the whiskey to the chilled egg-yolk mixture. With a rubber spatula, fold in the cooled egg whites and whipped cream. Blend well. Pour into a 10-inch soufflé mold or 10 individual 1-cup soufflé molds. Cover with plastic wrap and freeze 6 hours or overnight. Serve with Raspberry Coulis or fresh raspberries.

# Chocolate Brick

*A solid, dense chocolate lovers' dessert.*

**[Serves 8 to 10]**

24 ladyfingers

¾ cup (1½ sticks) unsalted
butter

Scant ½ cup sugar

½ cup unsweetened cocoa
powder

3 ounces bittersweet chocolate,
melted and cooled to
lukewarm

1½ cups heavy cream

2 tablespoons dark rum

Mocha Crème Anglaise
(page 78)

Line the sides of a 4½ × 8½ × 2½-inch loaf pan with the ladyfingers. It may be necessary to brush a light band of butter around the middle of the sides of the pan to keep the ladyfingers in place.

Place the butter in the bowl of an electric mixer and beat with the paddle attachment for 1 minute. Gradually add the sugar, continuing to beat until light and fluffy. Add the cocoa and beat for 2 minutes more. Add the chocolate and, using a rubber spatula, combine well. Whip the cream until soft peaks form. Add the rum and cream to the chocolate mixture and mix with the spatula until well combined. Pour into the prepared loaf pan. Chill for 4 hours or overnight.

Unmold onto a serving platter, if necessary running a thin-bladed knife around the inside of the pan to release the ladyfingers. Serve with Mocha Crème Anglaise.

# Triple Chocolate Terrine

*This dessert, composed of layers of white, milk,*
*and bittersweet chocolate surrounded by Raspberry Coulis,*
*is a classic combination of tastes.*

**[Serves 8 to 10]**

5 ounces white chocolate

5 ounces milk chocolate

5 ounces bittersweet chocolate

2¾ cups heavy cream

Double recipe Raspberry
Coulis (page 80)

Place flat on a work surface a length of plastic wrap, large enough to cover the bottom and sides of a 5 × 9-inch loaf pan. Place an equal-sized piece of plastic wrap on top and press together, smoothing out any air bubbles. Fit into the loaf pan. Set aside.

Chop the chocolates separately and place each in a medium metal bowl. Place the bowl of white chocolate over a *bain-marie* of hot, but not boiling, water, stirring frequently until melted. (White chocolate burns easily and must be watched.) Whip ¾ cup of the cream until soft peaks form. Fold the cream into the warm chocolate with a rubber spatula until no streaks show. Pour into the loaf pan and smooth the top with a spatula. Refrigerate. Repeat with the milk chocolate and ¾ cup of the cream, smoothing it over the white chocolate mixture. Repeat with the bittersweet chocolate and the remaining 1¼ cup of cream. If any streaks of chocolate show, use a wire whisk to smooth out the mixture. Smooth the bittersweet chocolate over the milk chocolate. Cover with plastic wrap and chill 4 hours or overnight.

Turn out on a serving platter and slice into 1-inch portions. Serve with some Raspberry Coulis spooned around each portion.

# Caramel Trifle

*You can put this wonderful dessert together in no time if the cake and sauces have been made ahead.*

[Serves 8 to 10]

1 10-inch Yellow Génoise (page 71)
⅓ cup rum
1 cup cold water
3 medium bananas
1 pint strawberries, wiped with a damp cloth, hulled and cut in half
1½ cups chopped walnuts
1 recipe Caramel Sauce (page 82)
1 double recipe Crème Anglaise (page 78)
4 cups heavy cream
2 tablespoons confectioners' sugar

Slice the *génoise* horizontally into 3 layers. Place one layer in a glass bowl, 10 inches in diameter and approximately 6 inches deep. Mix the rum and water and sprinkle one-third over the cake. Slice 1 banana thinly and spread over the cake in one layer. Put about one-third of the sliced berries around the bananas, then sprinkle with ½ cup of the nuts. Drizzle one-third of the Caramel Sauce over the fruit. Mix the Crème Anglaise with 2 cups of the cream and pour one-third of the mixture over the fruit. Break the second layer of *génoise* into 7 or 8 rough pieces. Place the pieces in the bowl and repeat the layers, using one-third of the rum syrup, fruit, nuts, Caramel Sauce, and Crème Anglaise. Break up the third layer of *génoise* and repeat with the remaining syrup, fruit, nuts, and sauces.

Whip the remaining cream with the confectioners' sugar until stiff peaks form. Spread all but ½ cup smoothly over the top of the trifle. Put the remaining cream into a pastry bag fitted with a ½-inch fluted tip and decorate the top of the trifle with rosettes. The top can also be sprinkled with some chopped walnuts and strawberries. Chill before serving.

**Note:** Candied violets also make a pretty decoration for the trifle.

# Pears Praline

*The crushed Nougatine showered over the
pears' meringue cream coating glitters like
small amber jewels.*

**[Serves 8]**

Juice of 1 lemon

2 cups water

2 cups dry white wine

½ cup sugar

8 ripe medium Bartlett pears,
peeled and cored

TO ASSEMBLE:

2 cups heavy cream

3 large egg whites

¼ cup sugar

¼ cup plus 2 tablespoons
Pear William
(eau-de-vie de poire)

1 recipe Yellow Génoise
(page 71) cut into 8
3-inch rounds, or
approximate size of
base of pears

2 cups crushed Nougatine
(page 83)

Combine the lemon juice, water, wine, and sugar in a 6-quart pot and bring to a boil over high heat. Boil for 5 minutes, then add the pears. Lower the heat to a simmer and continue cooking for 15 minutes or until the pears are tender. Chill the pears in the syrup. (This can be done the day before.)

One to 2 hours before serving, whip the cream until soft peaks form. Beat the egg whites until white and foamy while gradually adding the sugar. Continue beating the whites until stiff. Using a rubber spatula, fold in the whipped cream. Blend in 2 tablespoons of the Pear William.

Place each cake round on a dessert plate and brush with the remaining Pear William. Drain the pears and place each upright on a round. (You may need to cut a thin slice from the bottom of the pear to help it remain upright.) With a small metal spatula, cover the pears completely with the meringue mixture. Chill until ready to serve. Just before serving, sprinkle each pear generously with the crushed Nougatine. This should be done at the last minute to keep the nougat crunchy.

# Chocolate Bombe

*This dessert looks special yet takes little time to make if you have the* ganache *and toffee or Nougatine on hand.*

[Serves 8 to 10]

5 cups heavy cream

6 cups Crème Ganache (page 75)

3 to 4 tablespoons Grand Marnier

2 cups crushed Nougatine (page 83), or 2 cups crushed English Toffee (page 50)

1 tablespoon confectioners' sugar

Candied violets and spearmint leaves

Line a 9-inch round-bottomed bowl with a double thickness of plastic wrap, making sure the ends of the wrap extend over the edge of the bowl all the way around. Set aside.

Lightly whip 3 cups of the cream until soft peaks form. Chill the remaining cream for later use. Warm the *ganache* to room temperature by placing it in the bowl of an electric mixer and setting the bowl in a *bain-marie* of hot, but not boiling, water. Stir the *ganache* for about 1 minute. Remove the bowl from the *bain-marie* and with the whisk attachment of the electric mixer beat at medium-high speed until fluffy. The *ganache* should be room temperature and have a shiny finish. (If the *ganache* is too cold and firm, it will not combine well with the cream, in which case you may need to place the bowl in the hot water a few seconds more. If your bowl is metal it will hold the heat, so remove it a bit before you think the *ganache* will be ready.) When the ganache is the right texture, fold in the whipped cream with a rubber spatula and mix well. Fold in the Grand Marnier. Immediately pour half the mixture into the prepared mold and cover with a layer of crushed Nougatine or crushed toffee. Spoon in the rest of the mixture and smooth the top with a rubber spatula. Cover the surface with a piece of plastic wrap. Chill for 4 hours or overnight.

To unmold, remove the plastic wrap from the surface and invert the mold onto a 10- or 12-inch platter. Carefully lift off the plastic lining.

Smooth the surface of the bombe with a metal spatula dipped in hot water. Whip the remaining 2 cups of cream with the confectioners' sugar until stiff peaks form. Using a spatula, smooth all but ½ cup of the cream over the entire surface of the bombe. Place the remaining cream in a pastry bag fitted with a ½-inch fluted tip and swirl some rosettes on top of the bombe. Arrange candied violets and spearmint leaves around the rosettes.

# Red and White Parfait

*This is a delicate pudding of rice and almonds*
*with the added tartness of cranberry sauce. It looks*
*so tempting layered in glass goblets.*

[Serves 6]

1 cup sliced almonds

1 quart milk

3 tablespoons sugar

¾ cup long-grain white rice

¼ cup cream sherry

1 cup heavy cream, chilled

1 12-ounce bag fresh
   cranberries

1 cup water

1 cup sugar

Preheat the oven to 350° F.

Spread the almonds on a baking sheet and toast for approximately 10 minutes or just until they turn tan. Watch carefully, since almonds can burn quickly. Set aside.

Combine the milk and sugar in a 2-quart saucepan and bring to a boil over medium heat. Add the rice, stirring several times, then lower the heat and simmer uncovered for approximately 30 minutes, stirring occasionally. The mixture will be done when all the milk has been absorbed and there is no hard kernel in the center of a grain of rice. Pour the rice immediately into a medium-sized bowl to cool it quickly, then add the almonds and sherry and mix well. Cool the mixture to room temperature.

Place the cream in the bowl of an electric mixer, and whip with the whisk attachment until soft peaks form. Fold the cream into the rice. Chill the mixture while you make the cranberry sauce.

Rinse the cranberries under cold running water and pick over carefully. Place in a 2-quart saucepan with the sugar and water. Bring to a boil over medium heat and boil just until the cranberries have popped and the mixture has thickened, about 5 minutes. Cool to room temperature.

Alternately layer the rice and cranberries in glass goblets, starting and ending with the cranberries. Chill until ready to serve. Decorate with sprigs of mint, if you like.

# Master
# Recipes

*Yellow Génoise*

*Chocolate Génoise*

*Almond Génoise*

*Sweet Dough Pastry*

*Crème Ganache*

*Buttercream*

*Crème Anglaise*

*Lemon Cream Jean-Louis*

*Apricot Cream*

*Raspberry Coulis*

*Apricot Glaze*

*Caramel Sauce*

*Nougatine*

# Yellow Génoise

*A very basic cake to have on hand. The layers
serve as the base for many of the cold dessert recipes
in this book. Any leftover cake can easily
be frozen for later use.*

**[Makes one 10-inch cake]**

½ cup (1 stick) butter
6 large eggs
1 cup sugar
1 teaspoon vanilla extract
1 cup cake flour, sifted

Preheat the oven to 350° F. Butter and flour one 10-inch round cake pan.

Melt the butter in a small saucepan over low heat. When the butter is completely melted, skim the foam off the top with a small spoon, being careful not to disturb the milky residue on the bottom. Pour off the clear butter into another small pot and discard the residue. Keep the butter lukewarm.

Combine the eggs, sugar, and vanilla in a large stainless-steel mixing bowl. Fill a large pan with enough hot water to come at least 2 inches up the sides of the bowl and place over low heat. Put the bowl in the pan and whisk the egg mixture with a portable electric mixer on medium-high speed or hand whisk until it triples in volume and feels cool to the touch, about 8 to 10 minutes. Remove the bowl from the pan. Using a rubber spatula, fold in one-third of the flour, then one-third of the butter. Repeat twice more, using all the flour and butter. Don't overwork the batter or the cake will be tough and dry.

Pour the batter into the prepared pan and bake for 20 to 25 minutes, or until the top is lightly browned and the cake pulls away slightly from the sides of the pan. Let cool for about 5 minutes, then invert the cake onto a rack to cool completely. The cake can be used immediately, but it slices a little easier if it has been chilled for an hour or so.

# Chocolate Génoise

*This classic French recipe is very versatile.*
*It also freezes well.*

**[Makes one 10-inch round cake]**

½ cup (1 stick) unsalted butter
¾ cup cake flour, sifted
¼ cup unsweetened cocoa
    powder, sifted
6 large eggs
1 cup sugar

Preheat the oven to 350° F. Butter and flour a 10-inch round cake pan.

Melt the butter in a small saucepan over low heat. When the butter is completely melted, skim the foam off the top with a small spoon, being careful not to disturb the milky residue on the bottom. Pour off the clear butter into another small pot or bowl and discard the residue. Keep the butter lukewarm.

Sift the cake flour and cocoa together and set aside. Combine the eggs and sugar in a large stainless-steel mixing bowl. Fill a large pan with enough hot water to come at least 2 inches up the sides of the bowl and place over low heat. Put the bowl in the pan and whisk the mixture with a portable electric mixer at medium-high speed or hand whisk until it triples in volume and feels cool to the touch. Remove the bowl from the pan. Using a rubber spatula, fold in one-third of the flour and cocoa, then one-third of the butter. Repeat twice more until all the flour and butter are added.

Pour the batter into the prepared pan and bake for 20 to 25 minutes or until the top is lightly browned and the cake pulls away slightly from the sides of the pan. Let cool for about 5 minutes, then invert onto a rack to cool completely. Chill 1 hour before using.

# Almond Génoise

*This génoise is the base of the "Birdseed" Cake (page 14). It can also be used in place of the Chocolate Génoise (page 72).*

[Makes one 9½ × 13-inch rectangular cake]

1½ cups cake flour

2 tablespoons unsweetened cocoa

7 large eggs

1¼ cups sugar

4 ounces (½ can) almond paste, grated on the largest hole of a hand grater

2 tablespoons unsalted butter, melted and cooled to lukewarm

Preheat the oven to 350° F. Butter and flour the sides of a 9½ × 13 × 2½-inch baking pan. Line the bottom of the pan with parchment.

Sift together the flour and cocoa. Set aside. Combine the eggs and sugar in a large stainless-steel mixing bowl. Fill a large pan with enough hot water to come at least 2 inches up the sides of the bowl and place over low heat. Put the bowl in the pan and whisk the mixture with a portable electric mixer or a hand whisk until it triples in volume and feels cool to the touch.

Remove the bowl from the pan. Turn the mixer to the lowest speed and add the almond paste by the tablespoonful. (Don't worry if the batter doesn't look smooth after all the almond paste has been added.) Remove the bowl from the mixer and add one-third of the flour mixture, then one-third of the butter, folding in well with a rubber spatula after each addition. Repeat twice more until all of the flour and butter are added.

Pour the batter into the prepared pan and bake 20 to 25 minutes, or until the top is lightly brown and the cake pulls away slightly from the sides of the pan. Let the cake cool for about 5 minutes, then invert onto a rack to cool completely. Chill 1 hour before using.

# Sweet Dough Pastry

*This is my favorite recipe for pie and tart shells.*
*The dough rolls out easily and holds its shape during baking.*
*It will keep well for about one week in the refrigerator and*
*for two months in the freezer. If you're using a recipe*
*for a smaller tart or pie, any leftover dough*
*can be frozen for another use.*

[Makes one 10-inch pie or tart shell]

1¼ cups unsalted butter
1 cup confectioners' sugar, sifted
1 large egg
1 large egg yolk
1½ teaspoons vanilla extract
4 cups cake flour, sifted

Combine the butter and confectioners' sugar in the large bowl of an electric mixer and beat at low speed with the paddle attachment until well combined. Still at low speed, beat in the egg, egg yolk, and vanilla just until combined, then gradually add the flour in three parts. Mix just until the flour is barely combined. Finish mixing with a rubber spatula until well blended. Gather the dough into a ball, flatten slightly, and wrap in plastic wrap. Refrigerate for at least 1 hour.

Roll the dough out on a floured surface into a 12-inch circle, ⅛ inch thick. Dust the dough with flour, then carefully position the top end of the circle over the rolling pin and roll the entire circle onto the rolling pin toward you. Gently unroll the dough over the pan or tart shell. Dip your hands in flour and press the dough very gently down into the bottom and sides of the pan. Cut off any overhanging dough with a paring knife and prick the sides and bottom with a fork. Refrigerate for at least 1 hour.

Preheat the oven to 350° F. Cover the bottom and sides of the dough with a piece of aluminum foil and fill with dried beans or rice. For a partially baked shell, bake for 15 minutes only. For a fully baked shell, remove the foil after 15 minutes and continue baking until golden brown and firm. Cool shell before using a chilled filling.

# Crème Ganache

*This is probably one of the easiest, most useful,
and delicious recipes to have on file. It fills, covers, glazes,
and fulfills myriad chocolate fantasies. I'm calling for a
large quantity of ganache, but it keeps beautifully
in the refrigerator for a week or in the
freezer for several months.*

[Makes about 4 cups]

1 quart heavy cream

2 pounds bittersweet chocolate, chopped

Bring the cream to a boil in a 6-quart pot. When the cream boils up, immediately remove it from the heat and add the chocolate all at once. Stir with a wire whisk until the chocolate is melted, and continue to stir until the mixture is smooth and no small lumps of chocolate appear. Pour into a bowl, allow to cool at room temperature, cover with plastic wrap, and chill. Scoop out the needed amount with a metal spoon that has been dipped in hot water. This recipe can be doubled or tripled successfully.

# Buttercream

*I usually like two kinds of buttercream for
a layer cake, one made with egg whites, the other with
yolks. I prefer to use the egg yolk cream as filling because
it's silkier and richer. I use the meringue cream to cover the
cake, especially when I need a very pale color outside. I have
given the recipes for both buttercreams so that the eggs
can be used in tandem to avoid waste. If you have more
buttercream than you can use for one recipe (and you
probably will if you make both buttercreams), remember
that it freezes beautifully and can be thawed either
overnight in the refrigerator or for several
hours at room temperature.*

꧁꧂꧁꧂꧁꧂

## *Meringue Buttercream*

### [Makes about 1 quart]

12 large egg whites
2 cups sugar
½ cup water
4 cups (8 sticks) unsalted
butter, softened

Place the egg whites in the bowl of an electric mixer. Combine the sugar and water in a 1-quart saucepan and stir to mix well. Place over high heat and bring to a boil, stirring to dissolve the sugar. Wash any undissolved sugar crystals from the sides of the pan with a pastry brush dipped in cold water. While the sugar cooks, beat the egg whites at the lowest speed with the whisk attachment. The whites should be opaque and foamy at the same time that the sugar syrup reaches the firm ball stage or 242° F. on a candy thermometer. When the syrup is ready, remove it from the heat and immediately pour it into the egg whites, beating constantly at medium-high speed. Continue to beat until the whites are at room temperature, about 15 minutes. Lower the speed and add the butter, several tablespoons at a time, beating until all the butter has been incorporated and scraping down the sides of the bowl if necessary. If the buttercream seems too thin, beat in an additional ½ cup butter.

≈≈≈≈≈≈

# Egg Yolk Buttercream

### [Makes 3 cups]

12 large egg yolks

1 cup sugar

¼ cup water

2 cups (4 sticks) unsalted butter, softened

Follow the above directions for Meringue Buttercream. You will find that it is necessary to beat the egg yolks longer in order to bring them to room temperature before you add the butter. But this delicious cream is worth the extra effort.

# Crème Anglaise

*This sauce is the base for mousses and bavarians and can
also be used to cloak a variety of desserts.*

**[Makes about 3 cups]**

2 cups milk
5 large egg yolks
½ cup sugar

Place the milk in a heavy, nonreactive 2-quart
saucepan and bring to a boil over medium-
high heat. Place the egg yolks and sugar in a
medium bowl and whisk until very thick and
light in color. Gradually pour about 1 cup of the hot milk into the yolks,
whisking as you pour. Return the yolk mixture to the saucepan and stir
over low heat until thick enough to coat a wooden spoon. To test, dip the
spoon in the custard, then run your finger through the custard on the
spoon. The division made by your finger should remain. Immediately
remove from the heat and strain the mixture through a sieve into a
stainless-steel or glass bowl. Refrigerate, well covered, until ready to use.
This will keep for several days.

**Variation:** Mocha Crème Anglaise. Dissolve 2 tablespoons instant es-
presso powder in 2 tablespoons dark rum. Stir into cooled Crème Anglaise.

# Lemon Cream Jean-Louis

*Of all the lemon custard recipes I've tried, this one is my favorite because of its very tart, piquant flavor.*

[Makes 3 cups]

2 cups fresh lemon juice (about 10 large lemons); finely grate the zest of 5 of the lemons before making the juice

6 large eggs

6 large egg yolks

1½ cups sugar

1 cup (2 sticks) unsalted butter

Place the lemon juice, zest, and butter in a 4-quart, heavy-bottomed enamel or stainless-steel saucepan. Bring to a boil over medium heat. Remove from the heat. Mix the eggs, egg yolks, and sugar together in a medium-size bowl just until well combined. Do not beat. Add 1 cup of the butter mixture to warm the eggs, stir, then add to the remaining butter mixture. Stir with a whisk over medium-high heat until thick and smooth, about 5 to 8 minutes. Be sure to stir vigorously, touching all points of the bottom of the pot to make sure the mixture doesn't burn.

Strain into a stainless-steel or glass bowl. Place a layer of plastic wrap directly on the top of the cream to prevent a skin from forming. Cool at room temperature. Chill before using. This keeps for about 2 weeks in the refrigerator.

# Apricot Cream

*I love this filling between two layers of the*
*Gâteaux Bretonnes (page 44).*

[Makes about 1 cup]

2 tablespoons cornstarch
⅓ cup cream sherry
¾ cup apricot jam, puréed in a
blender or food processor
Juice and grated zest of 1
orange
2 tablespoons freshly squeezed
lemon juice

Combine the cornstarch and sherry in a 1-quart saucepan. Stir until smooth. Add the jam, orange juice, zest, and lemon juice. Cook over medium heat, stirring constantly until thick, about 4 minutes. Pour into a bowl and cover with a piece of plastic wrap. Chill several hours before using. This will keep in the refrigerator for 1 week.

# Raspberry Coulis

*Simple to make and an excellent accompaniment*
*to the Whiskey Mousse (page 59) and the Triple Chocolate*
*Terrine (page 61). If you use frozen berries,*
*try to get them without sugar.*

[Makes about 1 cup]

2 boxes (1 pint) fresh
raspberries, or 1 10-ounce
box frozen, thawed
Sugar
Freshly squeezed lemon juice

Purée the raspberries in a food processor, then pass through a sieve to remove the seeds. Add sugar and lemon juice to taste and stir to blend. Refrigerate until ready to serve.

# Apricot Glaze

*This can be used to brush a glistening coat on
various fruits and pastries.*

[Makes about 1 cup]

1 12-ounce jar apricot preserves
4 tablespoons calvados or Grand
  Marnier (calvados tastes best
  with apple desserts and Grand
  Marnier complements orange)

With the back of a large spoon, rub the preserves through a strainer or sieve that has been set over a 1-quart saucepan. Add the liqueur and cook over medium heat, stirring often, until thickened, about 8 minutes. If the glaze is not being used right away, cool to room temperature and store, covered, in the refrigerator. When ready to use, reheat to boiling. The glaze will keep in the refrigerator for 2 to 3 weeks.

# Caramel Sauce

*A luscious and versatile sauce to pour over*
*ice cream or use as a glaze for a fresh berry dessert.*
*The recipe can be easily doubled.*

[Makes about 1¼ cups]

1 cup sugar
½ cup water
1 cup heavy cream

Have ready a pastry brush, a long-handled wire whisk, and an oven mitt.

Combine the sugar and water in a 2-quart, heavy-bottomed saucepan, stirring well. Place over medium heat and bring to a boil. As the sugar is cooking, dip the pastry brush in cold water and wash down the sides of the pan to rinse away any undissolved sugar crystals. Continue to stir and wash down the sides of the pan until the sugar comes to a boil. As the sugar boils, move the pan gently back and forth over the burner to ensure even heat distribution. The sugar will turn golden, then nut-colored. When it smells like caramel and gives off little wisps of smoke, immediately remove it from the heat since the caramel will burn very quickly at this point. Put on the oven mitt, stand back a bit, and add the heavy cream very slowly, stirring rapidly as you pour. The sugar will bubble up and may splatter, but it will calm down as it cools. Serve at room temperature, or store in the refrigerator in a covered bowl or jar until ready to use. This will keep 1 week.

**Variation:** Ginger Caramel Sauce. Purée 2 ounces of preserved ginger with 1 tablespoon of the syrup it is packed in. Mix into hot Caramel Sauce. Serve on coffee ice cream showered with sliced, toasted almonds.

# Nougatine

*This versatile candy gives flavor and texture*
*to desserts such as the Pears Praline (page 63)*
*and is excellent sprinkled over ice cream.*
*It is best made on a dry day.*

[Makes about 5 cups]

2½ cups sugar

2 tablespoons light corn syrup

½ cup water

3 cups sliced almonds

Coat a jelly-roll pan with vegetable oil. Set aside.

Put the sugar, corn syrup, and water in a heavy 3-quart saucepan and stir until well combined. Place over medium heat and continue to stir until the sugar comes to a boil. As the mixture cooks, wash down the sides of the pan with a pastry brush dipped in cold water to rinse away any undissolved sugar crystals. Continue to boil without stirring, gently agitating the pan to distribute the heat. Watch carefully and remove the pan from the heat when you begin to see small puffs of smoke coming from the sugar, which should be dark brown but not burned. Quickly stir in the almonds, then pour onto the jelly-roll pan. Let cool.

When completely cool, place the nougatine in a sturdy plastic bag and break into small pieces with a hammer or heavy mallet. Store in an airtight container. It will keep for several weeks at room temperature.

# Index

‎~~~~~~‎